AGE DISCRIMINATION:
WEATHERING THE STORM

AGE DISCRIMINATION: WEATHERING THE STORM

WAYNE L. DAVIS, PH.D.
CHRISTOPHER ALLEN, MPA

Rev. date: 01/14/2015

To order additional copies of this book, contact:
Xlibris
1-888-795-4274
www.Xlibris.com
Orders@Xlibris.com
657052

Preface

This book may prove valuable to anyone who is interested in joining the Indiana State Police but who is currently over the department's maximum age limit for initial hire or rehire. This book contains information that may prove valuable to anyone who may decide to challenge the department's age-hiring policy in court. In addition, this book discusses ethical behaviors that impact police behaviors.

Authors

Wayne L. Davis, Ph.D.

Wayne L. Davis holds the following degrees: a Bachelor of Science in Electrical Engineering from the University of Michigan-Dearborn, a Master of Science in Business Administration from Madonna University, and a Ph.D. in Criminal Justice from Capella University. Dr. Davis has graduated from city, state, and federal law enforcement academies and has over 20 years of law enforcement experience with city, state, and federal law enforcement agencies. Dr. Davis was a field training officer with the Indiana State Police. In addition, Dr. Davis has received the U.S. Customs & Border Protection Scholastic Award and the U.S. Customs & Border Protection Commissioner's Award.

Dr. Davis has several academic and textbook publications. Dr. Davis teaches criminal justice and specializes in converting English logical statements (i.e., the law) into mathematical logical statements in order to determine the truth values of laws, police reports, and the actions of police officers and residents. In other words, Dr. Davis uses English and truth values (Boolean algebra) to articulate the legality of police actions.

Christopher Allen, MPA

Christopher Allen holds the following degrees: an Associate in Criminal Justice from Central Arizona College, a Bachelor in Criminal Justice from Ball State University, and a Master in Public Affairs from Indiana University. In addition, he has over 20 years of law enforcement experience with the Indiana State Police and with the Department of Corrections.

Davis   Allen

Table of Contents

List of Tables

List of Figures

Chapter 1

AGE DISCRIMINATION: CASE OF INDIANA STATE POLICE

Indiana State Police: Age Discrimination & Violation of Law

The following information may prove valuable to anyone who is interested in joining the Indiana State Police but who is currently over the department's maximum age for initial hire or rehire. Although the maximum age limit is currently 39 years of age, it used to be 34 years of age. Below is information that may prove valuable to anyone who may decide to challenge the department's age-hiring policy in court. **It only takes one person who has the resources and who is interested in challenging the Indiana State Police's age policy to change state practice.**

Table 1
Age Discrimination Case Synopsis (Davis v. Indiana State Police, 2008; Davis v. Whitesell, 2011).

Point	Chronological Actions	Perception of Police
1	1996 - The Indiana State Police (ISP) fired Christopher ALLEN at the Indiana State Police Academy because ALLEN had a brain tumor.	

2	Christopher ALLEN hired a lawyer and started a lawsuit against the ISP.	
3	The ISP provided medical records that ALLEN was unfit for duty.	
4	ALLEN never saw ISP doctors for the brain tumor and claimed that the medical records were false.	
5	ISP claimed to have destroyed/ lost ALLEN's personnel records.	
6	1998- The ISP rushed to rehire ALLEN and had a special ceremony to appoint ALLEN as a trooper (he was the only one appointed that day), but ALLEN was now over the department's maximum age limit for new hires.	
7	2005 – DAVIS leaves the ISP to join U.S. Dept. of Homeland Security.	
8	2006 – DAVIS seeks rehire with the ISP. DAVIS proceeds through the rehire process and is welcomed back as a trooper.	

9	Shortly thereafter, the ISP claims that DAVIS is too old and that something is in his background. DAVIS is denied rehire.	
10	DAVIS inquires about the "something in the background" but ISP does not respond.	
11	DAVIS must decide whether to file an age discrimination law suit in state or federal court. State Court – maximum age for new hires violates state law (Indiana Code 10-11-2-10) Federal Court – maximum age for new hires violates federal law (Age Discrimination in Employment Act, 29 U.S.C. §§ 621-33a)	
12	DAVIS files an age discrimination law suit against the ISP in federal court.	

13	2008 - U.S. 7th Circuit Court stated that wherever the law draws a line there will be cases on either side of the line that will be functionally indistinguishable, but that does not invalidate the line. In other words, if the ISP violated its age limit policy in the past, then the department's age policy cannot be enforced. In addition, the Court ruled that instead of the plaintiff proving that the department has violated the age policy, the police department must now show that it has not violated the policy (i.e., the burden of proof is now on the police department, who has control over the records). However, the U.S. 7th Circuit also ruled that under federal law, a bona fide policy may be senseless and may violate state law (in other words, statutory law cannot be conflated to constitutional criteria).	

14	DAVIS subpoenaed his personnel records, all electronic records related to the case, and the hiring records of the ISP to determine the age of new hires. The ISP claimed to have destroyed/lost the personnel records of DAVIS and all electronic records related to the case.	
15	The ISP only provided partial information on its hiring practices.	
16	ISP officers were deposed and the "something in the background" was dropped. Age was stated to be the sole factor for failing to rehire Davis. Several key Indiana State Police officers all claimed to have been unable to remember fundamental details when they were deposed. By doing this, they did not have to provide any information that may have been detrimental to their case.	
17	The ISP admitted to the U.S. 7th Circuit Court that the department hired ALLEN over the age limit. However, the department claimed that it was a clerical mistake.	

18	2011- The U.S. 7th Circuit Court ruled that the ISP made a good faith mistake and that DAVIS did not prove his case (the Court's decision did not consider the point that ALLEN was a special appointment because that fact was not brought up).	

Indiana State Police Age Discrimination Case

During the Indiana State Police Academy in October 1996, Christopher Allen was told by his personal doctor in Carmel, Indiana that he had a benign brain tumor. His doctor stated that it could be removed and, once removed, Allen would be able to perform all police duties. Allen reported this fact to the Indiana State Police, who stated that it was no big deal. However, in November 1996, the Indiana State Police told Allen to quit or he would be fired. Allen refused to quit, so he was fired.

Allen had surgery and had the brain tumor removed in January 1997. Soon afterward, Allen stated that the Indiana State Police had produced medical records from its affiliated doctor, who claimed that Allen was unfit for duty. Allen filed a lawsuit and challenged the medical records because Allen had never seen the department's affiliated doctor. In other words, the Indiana State Police had produced false medical records. The Indiana State Police realized that they were in trouble when Allen's lawyer requested all of their records. Subsequently, the Indiana State Police claimed to have destroyed/lost Allen's personnel records.

After Allen had challenged the medical records during his lawsuit, the Indiana State Police had a special appointment and re-hired Allen. Allen was the only trooper that the Indiana State Police hired on that particular day, which was February 2, 1998. The Indiana State Police hired Allen after he had already passed the maximum age limit for rehire. In 2011, the Indiana State Police stated to the U.S. 7th Circuit Court during the *Davis v. Indiana State Police/Whitesell* case that Allen was hired over the maximum age limit. However, the Indiana State Police claimed that Allen was hired over the age limit due to a clerical error because they have hired thousands of employees and that Allen simply slipped through the cracks due to a clerical error. Again, Allen was a special appointment and he was the only trooper hired on February 2, 1998, which can be verified via Indiana State Police records.

In 2005, Wayne Davis left the Indiana State Police and joined the U.S. Department of Homeland Security. After about two months with the U.S. Department of Homeland Security, Davis wanted to return to the Indiana State Police. Davis applied to the Indiana State Police, passed all of the tests (e.g., polygraph, physical, psychological), and was welcomed back to the Indiana State Police. Shortly thereafter, the Indiana State Police stated that Davis was over the maximum age limit for new hires and that he would not be rehired.

Davis challenged the department's age limit in federal court (*Davis v. Indiana State Police*, 2008; *Davis v. Whitesell*, 2011). The U.S. District Court ruled against Davis. Davis appealed the case to the U.S. 7th Circuit Court. The 7th Circuit Court ruled that Davis had the right to collect Indiana State Police records to see if the department had made exceptions to its age hiring practice in the past. Davis subpoenaed all of the records; he wanted to know the age of all cadets at the time they were hired. The Indiana State Police resisted. The Indiana State Police claimed to have destroyed/lost many of Davis' personnel records and all of the electronic records related to the case. In addition, the Indiana State Police refused to turn over all of the subpoenaed documents that they did possess. Several years later, the Indiana State Police still only produced about half of the subpoenaed hiring records. The Indiana State Police provided Davis with about 1,170 records, but they clearly indicated to the U.S. 7th Circuit Court that there were thousands of records.

The records that the Indiana State Police did provide were cross-referenced against the Indiana State Police yearbooks and much of the information that was subpoenaed was missing. Davis' lawyer filed several motions with the U.S. District Court for the Indiana State Police to provide the rest of the information. The Indiana State Police refused to comply with the subpoena. Subsequently, the U.S. District Court ruled for the state, stating that Davis had failed to obtain enough information to prove his case. In the end, Davis failed to get a jury trial and his case was dismissed because he had failed to obtain enough information to prove his case (he never did get all of the subpoenaed information). The U.S. 7th Circuit Court did not say that Davis was wrong, only that he had failed to prove his case. Had Davis argued the following points in the appropriate court, the results may have been different.

Table 2

Legal Issues not Addressed in the Davis Case that may be argued in a future Court Case

Item	Legal Issues not Addressed in the Davis Case	Appropriate Court
1	ISP hiring practice is not in compliance with Indiana state law (Indiana Code 10-11-2-10) (LexisNexis, 2008; Office of Code Division, n.d.). Only about a dozen states have maximum age limit policies for new hires.	State

2	ISP had a special appointment and hired Christopher Allen while he was over the ISP maximum age limit, which was 34 years of age at the time. He was the only one hired on February 2, 1998, which can be verified via ISP hiring records. This demonstrates that the hiring of Allen was not a clerical error (ISP argued that the department hired thousands of employees and that Allen slipped through the cracks).	Federal
3	At least two Superintendents were hired over the maximum age limit. Superintendent Whitesell patrolled the highways as a state police officer. A Superintendent can be hired from within the department. Indiana Code 10-11-2-6 does not excuse the Superintendent from meeting the age requirement ("Indiana Code", 2014).	State/Federal
4	The ISP new hire maximum age limit is not a constant. The ISP maximum age limit for new hires changed from 34 to 39 years of age around 2005. The increase in age allowed certain individuals to be hired who were currently over the age limit. The U.S. 7th Circuit Court ruled that a bona fide age policy cannot be spun for an occasion (Davis v. Indiana State Police, 2008).	Federal

In short, the poor person has little chance against a large police department. For example, it was a good defense strategy for the Indiana State Police to drag out the *Davis* case for almost 5 years, fighting to keep a jury from hearing the case. Individuals with limited financial resources may be forced to drop their cases against the department due to the high cost of legal fees (or the defendants may die or move away and lose interest). It would have been much faster and cost effective to let the *Davis* case go to a jury trial. However, the Indiana State Police did not want the case to go to trial because they knew the truth would come out. In other words, the only way the Indiana State Police could have won the case was to not let a jury hear the case. If the department had lost the case, there might have been a significant cost to the department to restructure its pension program.

In addition, when the Indiana State Police officers were deposed and caught in less than competent/truthful situations, they simply responded that they did not remember how they made their decisions and that they had no documentation to refresh their memories. In other words, saying that they "do not remember" is a technique used by police officers to escape bad situations. In this way, they can always remember select information later, when it is convenient, without contradiction. This will be hard for a plaintiff to overcome.

Table 3
Davis Case Points of Interest

Item	Points of Interest
1	Indiana State Police claimed to have destroyed/lost personnel records related to the case. In sum, there were about 25 different letters of recognition and commendation that had disappeared from Davis' file, which one Indiana State Police administrator stated was disturbing.
2	Indiana State Police claimed to have destroyed/lost all electronic records related to the case.

3	Indiana State Police failed to produce all hiring records.
4	Indiana State Police had a special appointment for Christopher Allen, who was over age limit for new hires.
5	Superintendents who were over the age limit have been appointed to the ISP (the law can be satisfied if the Superintendent is appointed from within the department).
6	The ISP maximum age limit for new hires is illegal because it does not comply with the age policies of most other states (Indiana Code 10-11-2-10) (LexisNexis, 2008; Office of Code Division, n.d.).

Conclusion

The Indiana State Police has not always followed its age hiring policy. Indeed, the Indiana State Police had a special appointment and hired Christopher Allen, who they knew was over the maximum age limit for new hires. Allen was the only trooper that the department appointed on February 2, 1998 and he was over the age limit. However, the Indiana State Police stated to the U.S. 7th Circuit Court that hiring Allen over the maximum age limit was a clerical mistake (*Davis v. Indiana State Police*, 2011). The Indiana State Police Department had to say that because making an exception to its age hiring policy would have voided the policy. Although Davis failed to prove his case, this does not mean that Davis was wrong. Another person can follow up and challenge the Indiana State Police's maximum age hiring policy in either federal or state court.

References

Davis v. Indiana State Police, 541 F.3d 760 (7th Cir. September 3, 2008).

Davis v. Whitesell, No. 10-2617 (7th Cir. July 5, 2011).

Indiana Code - Section 10-11-2-6: Appointment of superintendent (2014). Retrieved from http://codes.lp.findlaw.com/incode/10/11/2/10-11-2-6

LexisNexis (2008). *Indiana criminal and traffic law manual.* Charlottesville, VA: Matthew Bender.

Office of Code Division Indiana legislature Services Agency (n.d.). *IC 10-11-2-10. Rank, grade, and position classifications.* Retrieved from http://www.in.gov/legislative/ic/2010/title10/ar11/ch2.html

Chapter 2

ETHICAL SYSTEMS & POLICE DEPARTMENT ORIENTATIONS

Proper Police Behavior

Why do police departments and their officers act in the ways that they do? Police actions are influenced by what the police department and the individual officers consider as good behavior. However, good behavior is relative and much conflict can develop when a police department's definition of good behavior differs from the officers' and/or residents' definition of good behavior.

Residents are Stakeholders

According to the Declaration of Independence, the U.S. government derives its power from the individuals that it governs (Hames & Ekern, 2005). Indeed, because there are about 400 U.S. residents for every full-time sworn police officer, law enforcement requires that people voluntarily comply with the law and assist with law enforcement efforts (Reaves, 2007; U.S. Department of Labor, 2009). Furthermore, because the Posse Comitatus Act of 1878 generally prohibits the U.S. military from engaging in domestic law enforcement, and because the U.S. Constitution protects the public against unreasonable searches and seizures (i.e., protects privacy), local police are ill equipped to handle the crime problem alone (Brinkerhoff, 2009). Residents are stakeholders in maintaining a peaceful society and they must take an active part in promoting pro-social behaviors (Carter, 2002). However, the definition of good behaviors is relative. In short, before individuals can promote pro-social behaviors, a reference point is needed to define good behavior.

Test of Ethics

There is a test of ethics. First, the end must be justified as good (e.g., the conviction of criminals) (Pollock, 2004). Second, the means must be a plausible way to achieve the ends (e.g., police officers must articulate their actions). Third, there is no less intrusive method to achieve the same end (e.g., instead of strip searching drug smugglers, U.S. Customs officers could X-ray the suspects). Finally, the means must not undermine some other equal or greater end (e.g., community members must not lose faith in the legal system).

Table 4
Canons of Ethics (Christian Police & Prison Association, n.d.).

Canons of Ethics

- Officers shall uphold the Constitution
- Officers shall use ethical procedures
- Officers shall discharge duties as a public trust
- Officers shall conduct their private lives with integrity
- Officers shall hold freedom as a paramount precept
- Officers shall maintain the integrity and competence of the profession
- Officers shall cooperate with other officials to achieve law enforcement objectives
- Officers shall observe confidentiality
- Officers shall not compromise their integrity by accepting gratuities

Ethical Dilemmas

Ethical dilemmas arise as a result of conflicting core ethical values and may be inherent in some situations (Perez & Moore, 2002). Situations that involve unfair advantage, conflicts between personal values and institutional goals, power differentials, abuse of power, breaches of confidentiality, hidden agendas, impropriety or boundary violations, multiple roles, and differences in perceptions may generate ethical dilemmas. Ethical dilemmas can sometimes be foreseen by evaluating if particular signals exist. These signals may involve whether laws or professional standards are violated, whether there is internal conflict and doubt about the issue, whether anyone can be harmed as a result of the decision, whether the decision is objective, whether there is strong opposition to the decision, whether the decision can be revealed without hesitation, and whether anyone else would be willing to make the decision. When conflict arises, professional, social, and economic pressures can make ethical decision-making difficult.

Integrity has many gray areas and is a complex subject that is not always easily defined. Generally, however, integrity is a positive, proactive system of values that is constant over time and consists of fairness, honesty, sincerity, and doing what seems to be the proper thing (Dreisbach, 2008; Harberfeld, 2006; Hess & Bennett, 2007). Several standards that may be used to evaluate the integrity of police conduct are a) fair access, b) public trust, c) safety and security versus enforcement, d) teamwork, and e) objectivity. Fair access relates to fair and open access of police services to all citizens. Public trust relates to the trust that the civilians give to the police officers in exchange for their right to enforce laws. Safety and security versus enforcement relates to police officers using discretion in balancing the goal of maintaining order with the goal of enforcing the law. Teamwork relates to police officers who are expected to coordinate, communicate, and cooperate with others in the law enforcement system. Objectivity relates to police officers who are expected to be impartial and a disinterested party.

Ethical Systems – What is Good Behavior?

Ethics is the study of human conduct in the light of set ideas of right and wrong (i.e., morals) (Pollock, 2004). However, there are different ideas of right and wrong in which to judge good behavior. Consequently, different ethical systems answer the question, *"What is good?"* in different manners. **Moral principles** are set ideas of right and wrong that form the basis of ethical behaviors.

Deontological ethical system is concerned with the intent of the actor or goodwill as the element of morality (Pollock, 2004). The consequence of the action is unimportant. For example, the assassination of Hitler might be unethical under a deontological system because killing is always wrong. For police officers, shooting a murderer who is about to kill again is unethical.

Teleological ethical system is concerned with the consequences of an action to determine goodness (Pollock, 2004). For example, the assassination of Hitler might be ethical under a teleological system because the consequence may save many lives. For police officers, shooting a murderer who is about to kill again is ethical because it may save innocent lives.

Each ethical system answers the question, "What is good?" (Pollock, 2004). In other words, good behavior is relative and depends on the reference system (i.e., morals) used to judge behavior. For example, a behavior may be considered good according to one ethical system and bad according to another ethical system. However, not all behaviors are subject to ethical judgment; only those behaviors that are performed by humans acting with free will and that impact other people are subject to ethical judgment. In addition, a particular act may be defined as bad behavior for one person but not bad behavior for another person. For example, a child under the age of reason and a person that is mentally incapacitated may lack the knowledge and intent of wrong doing. Therefore, good behavior is relative. In addition, although personal values may influence individual moral beliefs and behaviors, not all personal values have ethical components. For example, the act of valuing one color automobile over another is ethically neutral and is based solely on personal opinion.

Criteria are used to decide what is right or wrong (Pollock, 2004). There are various ethical systems that use different criteria to evaluate the morality of an action. Some of the basic ethical systems that shape moral and ethical principles include 1) ethical formalism, 2) utilitarianism, 3) act utilitarianism, 4) rule utilitarianism, 5) religious ethics, 6) natural law, 7) ethics of virtue, 8) ethics of care, 9) egoism, 10) enlightened egoism, 11) ethical relativism, 12) cultural relativism, and 13) situational ethics.

Ethical formalism ethical system states that good is defined by a person's goodwill and by doing one's duty (Pollock, 2004). Good actions are based on categorical imperatives: (a) act as if the behavior will become a universal law, (b) do not use people for one's own purposes, and (c) act consistent with universal laws. For example, a lie is only a lie if the recipient is led to believe or has a right to believe that he or she is being told the truth. For instance, not telling a car thief that a bait car is being used to capture car thieves is not unethical. However, ethical formalism is problematic when there are conflicting duties (e.g., judge's order versus department policy).

Utilitarianism ethical system determines the goodness of an act by a benefit-to-cost ratio (Kraska, 2004; Pollock, 2004). The needs of the many outweigh the needs of the few. In other words, as the benefit-to-cost ratio increases, the better the act will be perceived. For example, it is okay to arrest innocent people by mistake if it solves a bigger problem.

Act Utilitarianism ethical system determines the goodness of a particular act by measuring the utility of the specific act without regard for future acts (Pollock, 2004). For example, it is not unethical to steal food when a person is hungry and has no other way to get food.

Rule Utilitarianism ethical system determines the goodness of an act by measuring the utility of the act when made into a rule for behavior (Pollock, 2004). For example, it is unethical to steal food when a person is hungry and has no other way to get food because this will result in lawlessness if people are allowed to steal food anytime that they are hungry and cannot afford food. Likewise, it may be unethical not to engage in high speed chases because this may encourage people to flee.

Religious ethics ethical system determines the goodness of an act based on the concepts of good and evil and what is good is based on God's will (Pollock, 2004). Ethics are determined by individual conscious, religious authorities, and Holy Scripture. However, problems with religious ethics are that no one may ever know exactly what the will of God is and there are current controversies within and between religions. For example, it may not be unethical or illegal for Native Americans to consume contraband mushrooms for religious practices.

An example of a controversy within religion is the use of deceit to save a life. For example, should a person lie to save an innocent child who is being sought by a gunman? Some Christian thinkers may argue for the existence of a higher ethic, namely love, and that lying to save a life is okay because it is based on good intent and love (Father F. Rogers, personal communication on 6/26/2014). If one looks at this situation as the *lesser of two evils*, then the greatest evil would be to contribute to the intended victim's death. In this case, if a lie allows the intended victim to get away safely, or if the gunman's threat can be neutralized, then a lie would be the *lesser of two evils*. The lie would have the effect of preserving life, which is a greater good and, therefore, justified.

However, from a biblical perspective, one does not have to answer the gunman's question at all (Father F. Rogers, personal communication on 6/26/2014). A person can choose to remain silent and to face the consequences. In this case, a person may choose to die rather than to sin by lying or by contributing to the harm of another person. Hence, one need not lie. In Christian ethics, self-preservation is not the ultimate good. Indeed, death is preferable to sin.

Natural law ethical system states that there is a universal set of rights and wrongs but without reference to specific supernatural beings (Pollock, 2004). What is good is determined by what is natural to humans (e.g., socialization and the right to life) and is free of passion. Indeed, the founding fathers might be described as natural law practitioners. However, identifying what is consistent and congruent with natural inclinations of humankind is a fundamental problem of this ethical system. This is evidenced by the changing of laws (e.g., marijuana use) and the development of new laws.

Ethics of virtue ethical system determines the goodness of an act based on the attempt to achieve happiness, such as living a good life and achieving life's goals (Pollock, 2004). Good behavior is based on the golden mean, which is the median between extreme states of character. For example, absolute police powers and civil liberties oppose one another. Effective law enforcement must compromise between the two. It is based on a person's character and includes factors such as honesty, humility, and temperance.

Ethics of care ethical system determines the goodness of an act based on meeting needs and preserving and enriching relationships (Pollock, 2004). Actions are taken based on connecting with other people, caring for the needs of other people, and being aware of other people. For example, involving a single event in which battery threats are made, instead of arresting the offender for intimidation (a felony), the police officer may arrest the offender for disorderly conduct (a misdemeanor), provocation (a civil infraction), or simply separate the parties (a warning). By taking the minimum enforcement action necessary in order to achieve peace, relationships will be enhanced and labeling may be prevented.

Egoism ethical system claims that good results from pursuing self-interests (Pollock, 2004). However, every person acting in his or her own best interests is not logical or feasible and this will result in great conflict. An example of egoism in law enforcement is when police officers write unnecessary tickets in order to meet quotas for good performance reviews.

Enlightened egoism claims that it is in one's long-term best interest to help others so that they will learn to help themselves (Pollock, 2004). For example, a police officer may refuse to change a flat tire on a car occupied with capable adults and may instead instruct them on how to change the tire themselves. Having the occupants change the tire themselves may prove valuable in the future if they get another flat tire and no assistance is available. However, community members may expect the police to provide full and immediate service and this may result in complaints. As a way to comply with departmental policy, police officers in the field may offer full service in terms of providing a wrecker service. If drivers are dissatisfied with that response due to time and cost, this may damage police-community relations.

Ethical relativism ethical system determines what is good or bad based on the individual or group (Pollock, 2004). For example, community members in a poor region may hunt and fish without purchasing the proper licenses. Likewise, prostitution may be encouraged and institutionalized in certain communities.

Cultural relativism defines good as that which contributes to the health and survival of society (Pollock, 2004). For example, men in certain cultures may kill their spouses if their wives expose their faces to strangers. However, U.S. law enforcers may sometimes need to identify these females. This conflict of interest is often encountered at the U.S. borders.

Situational ethics ethical system states that there are few universal truths and that different situations call for different responses (Pollock, 2004). Thus, the same action may be right in some situations and wrong in other situations. For example, it may be ethical for a person to violate the speed laws if he or she is racing an injured person to the hospital. However, the same action may be unethical if no such emergency exists.

Deceiving Suspects: Is it ethical for police officers to lie to suspects in the field?

Ethical Formalism: condemned, due to violation of categorical imperative; lying would become rule for all people

Religious: condemned, God is truth; possibly justified, if person can argue that it is the lesser of two evils

Rule Utilitarianism: condemned, because it may undermine long-term system of laws

Utilitarianism: justified, if benefits outweigh costs to society as a whole

Natural Law: justified, as long as civil rights are not violated

Ethics of Virtue: justified, if crimes are severe and if methods are moderate

Ethics of Care: justified, if it protects victims

Egoism: justified, if it is profitable to the police officer

Cultural Relativism: justified, as long as accepted by culture

Situational Ethics: justified, if police officer can effectively articulate reasons for deception in this particular case (evaluated on a case-by-case basis)

Ethics in Law Enforcement		
Utilitarianism Good is based on a benefit-cost ratio. Example of good behavior: arresting an innocent person in order to deter crime in general. 	**Types of Ethical Systems** • **Ethical Formalism** • **Utilitarianism** • **Religious** • **Natural Law** • **Ethics of Virtue** • **Ethics of Care** • **Egoism** • **Cultural Relativism** • **Situational Ethics**	**Ethics in Law Enforcement** **What is good behavior?** *Ethics is the study of set ideas of right and wrong. However, there are different ideas of right and wrong in which to judge good behavior. Consequently, different ethical systems answer the question, "What is good?" in different manners.*
Religious Good is based on God's will. Example of good behavior: always providing complete and truthful information, regardless of the cost. 	**Ethical Formalism** Good is based on goodwill and intent. Example of good behavior: catching a fleeing felon, even if the violator gets hurt. 	

Figure 1. Types of ethical systems.

Ethics in Law Enforcement		
Natural Law Good is based on a universal set of rights (i.e., what is natural). Example of good behavior: acting in accordance with the U.S. Constitution. 	**Ethics of Care** Good is based on the needs of those concerned. Example of good behavior: always arresting males who are involved in domestic violence in order to protect female victims. 	**Cultural Relativism** Good is based on what promotes the health and survival of society. Example of good behavior: Middle Eastern women refusing to show their faces in public. 
Ethics of Virtue Good is based on compromise. Example of good behavior: using non-intrusive X-Ray machines to search for contraband. 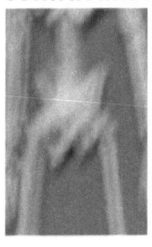 X-Ray	**Egoism** Good is based on what benefits the actor. Example of good behavior: writing a lot of tickets to meet the monthly quota for a good performance review. 	**Situational Ethics** Good is based on the particular situation at a particular time. Example of good behavior: speeding in order to get to the hospital to save a life. 

Figure 1 (continued). Types of ethical systems.

Ethical Systems Conclusion

The government derives its powers with the consent of the people (Cain, 2003). Indeed, the police can only govern the people if the people agree to be governed. Thus, the police must have a good relationship with the public. It is important that the community members respect the police. When police officers misbehave, they make a statement that forms an image of the officers. If a negative image is created by officers, then this will weaken the bond between the police and the public. Indeed, the officers must have integrity and the public must perceive that the officers have integrity. In this way, police-community relations will be enhanced and this will promote public safety.

Police Department Orientations

Eight theoretical orientations have been identified that describe the lenses in which police department administrators perceive crime and the criminal justice system (Kraska, 2004). See Figure 6. The orientation that a police department follows will influence how patrol officers act toward the public. The eight orientations include 1) Rational, 2) System, 3) Crime Control versus Due Process, 4) Politics, 5) Growth Complex, 6) Social Constructionist, 7) Oppression, and 8) Late Modernity. Having a reference point in which to evaluate good behavior will influence the actions of police officers in the field. However, each orientation is based on assumptions, which must be understood. The eight orientations are described below.

Rational Orientation

The rational orientation simply views law enforcement as a business. Peace and security can be achieved by controlling crime, and crime can be controlled by punishing offenders (Kraska, 2004). In other words, everyone is expected to follow the rules in order to achieve the agreed upon end result, which is peace. When a man, for example, decides not to follow the rules, he creates a tear in the fabric of peace, and this fabric must be repaired, which requires a cost. By not following the rules, this man has encroached upon the rights of other individuals and is forcing them to pay a cost for which he is responsible. Because this is not fair, laws are required to balance things out. The offender must pay a cost high enough, not only to repair the damage, but to deter him from disrupting social order in the future. If the penalty is not high enough to discourage future acts of deviance, then the public's confidence in public safety will be undermined. The greater the cost is to the public, the greater the cost that must be paid by the offender.

The main assumptions of the rational orientation are that everyone in society has equal value, everyone is in alignment, and everyone concedes to follow the agreed upon rules. It assumes that everyone has given up a little bit of personal freedom so that the government can enforce the agreed upon rules in order to promote public safety in a fair and impartial manner (Kraska, 2004). It assumes that crime has a cost and can be managed through payment.

System Orientation

The system orientation views criminal justice as an entity that consists of interacting, yet independent, agencies (Kraska, 2004). The various agencies function by drawing inputs from the external environment, transforming these inputs, and then sending the final product back into the environment as socially approved output. An example would be to collect convicts (input), to rehabilitate them through behavior modification programs (transform), and then to release them back into society (output). The system's independent units strive to maintain balance and internal stability as they sustain each other. It is believed that crime is a rational choice and that the size and power of the system must be increased in order accommodate increases in the crime rate.

The primary purpose of the criminal justice system, according to the system orientation, is to control crime via interagency cooperation (Kraska, 2004). It is believed that public safety can be achieved through efficient operations of each unit of the criminal justice system, including the legislative, executive, judicial, and correctional agencies. In this way, accused persons can be processed, rehabilitated, and returned to society in an effective and efficient manner that promotes social peace.

The main assumption of the system orientation is that those who have legal authority are capable of making rational decisions, which will reduce crime in an efficient manner (Kraska, 2004). It is believed that the system can adapt itself to accommodate changes in the external environment, usually by increasing its resources. By effectively and efficiently using resources and technology, by improving laws and policies, by improving judicial processes, and by improving rehabilitation and re-entry programs, it is expected that crime can be better controlled and public safety will be enhanced.

Crime Control Orientation versus Due Process Orientation

The main purpose of the crime control orientation is to secure peace by arresting as many law violators as possible, as fast as possible, and by using as few resources per arrest as possible (Kraska, 2004). Furthermore, because the defendants are presumed guilty (otherwise they would not have been arrested), releasing suspects due to procedural mistakes is wrong. In other words, suspects are guilty of their alleged crimes, otherwise law enforcement authorities would not spend the resources trying to prosecute the person (i.e., effective crime control does not focus on innocent people). It is believed that this quantitatively based tough-on-crime policy can be achieved by efficiently processing offenders informally and consistently through the legal system. This requires having few constitutional restraints placed upon law enforcers. However, the crime control orientation assumes that law enforcers a) are trustworthy and will enforce laws in a fair and legal manner, and b) can competently reconstruct crime scenes and develop the most accurate account of the actual events in a descriptive and factual manner. In short, mistakes are tolerated up to the point where they start to interfere with the suppression of crime.

The main purpose of the due process orientation is to protect people's rights by placing constraints upon the government and by making government officials defend their investigative procedures in an adversarial courtroom (Kraska, 2004). Due process advocates believe that mistakes are unacceptable, individual freedom is more valuable than absolute security, and that factual guilt does not equate to legal guilt. However, unless a person is provided the opportunity to present evidence, it is assumed that this distinction will not be made. This qualitative based policy assumes that the defendant will be provided adequate legal representation in the courtroom and that the legal system will lead to the discovery of the truth (e.g., whether the police honored procedural safeguards, as guaranteed by law). Indeed, the due process orientation requires that an unbiased third party make an objective evaluation of legal guilt.

Due process advocates view criminal justice as a necessary means to protect social freedom by protecting all citizens from unjust acts committed by government officials (Kraska, 2004). Because the cost of being incarcerated is extremely high, the due process orientation requires that the state eliminate all doubt as to whether constitutional procedural safeguards were violated. In order to control law enforcers, there must be a cost for violating the rules. Thus, in order to ensure that police officers will comply with the law, it is argued that the cost of releasing all suspects whose rights have been violated will be a high enough cost to motivate law enforcers to obey the law when they perform their duties. According to the due process orientation, corrupt police officers will cause the crime control orientation to fail.

Politics Orientation (Right Wing versus Left Wing)

According to the politics orientation, the criminal justice system is interest-based and its primary purpose is contingent upon the political climate at the time, which constantly changes according to who are in power (Kraska, 2004). Many interests groups fight for power and want to protect their own self-interests. Through negotiations, the different groups can protect their interests through checks and balances. This promotes an orderly offender processing system via rational policies. Politics, however, has two sides, a right wing and a left wing.

The right wing is conservative and the left wing is liberal (Kraska, 2004). On the one hand, the right wing believes that a) the system is too lenient with offenders, b) the system favors the rights of offenders over the rights of victims, c) youths no longer respect authorities, d) hard working law-abiding Americans are paying the high cost for crime, and e) society is too permissive involving morality issues. The left wing, on the other hand, believes that a) the system inappropriately includes certain vices as crimes, which indicates a more serious crime problem than really exists, b) authorities label people as criminals, which may stigmatize them and create a self-fulfilling prophecy, c) correctional facilities are warehouses for criminals and they fail to rehabilitate inmates, which lead to recidivism, d) centralized power discourages the involvement of community members in solving local problems, and e) the criminal justice system discriminates against and segregates minorities in order to control them.

The right wing and the left wing each have their own set of assumptions (Kraska, 2004). The right wing's assumptions state that a) people are responsible for their own actions, b) strong morals, based on a religious foundation, are essential for a healthy and well-functioning society, c) people have the right to be safe and secure in the areas where they spend most of their time, d) a healthy society requires that people obey the laws, which will be administered fairly and firmly, and e) social order requires that major categories of persons be segregated so that they can be controlled. The left wing's assumptions state that a) the primary cause of crime lies in dysfunctional social conditions, b) obsolete morality regulations are deficient in meeting the current needs of a majority of the population, c) there is an unequal distribution of power and resources in the country, d) a healthy society cannot discriminate against major categories of persons, e) official authorities stigmatize offenders by labeling them as criminals, which will lead to hardship and future crime, and f) the crime problem is exaggerated (thus, legal codes should be changed so that victimless crimes are not counted toward the crime problem).

Growth Complex Orientation

According to the growth complex orientation, the purpose of the criminal justice system is to build an ever growing bureaucracy; administering justice and controlling crime are tools that are used to increase the agency's size and power (Kraska, 2004). In an effort to meet the organizational ends in the most efficient way, scientific methods are established in order to create rules and regulations, which will get everyone to perform their duties in the same technically efficient and predictable manner. Instead of focusing on the outcome (doing the right thing), the rules and regulations become the standard for performance. Using statistics allows police departments to defend their enforcement practices. When someone challenges their apparently unfair enforcement tactics, the police can claim that individuals are arrested based on objective numeric analysis. They may also argue that without using statistics to classify and sentence people, each person's fate would be inconsistent and uncertain.

Operating under the growth complex orientation, there is an incentive to lock people up. Part of the criminal justice system has become privatized and many investors hope to profit (Kraska, 2004). On the one hand, the investors create many jobs. For example, workers are needed to build prisons, supply prison food, supply prison clothes, and provide medical care. On the other hand, the investors need customers (i.e., inmates); hence, there is an incentive to confine people in prison. By locking people up in prison, the state effectively manages the surplus labor force, which is naturally generated in a capitalistic society (Kraska, 2004). Thus, politicians appear to be effectively serving the public. After all, jobs are created and there are fewer unemployed people in the marketplace.

The main assumptions of the growth complex orientation are that a) a bureaucracy needs to survive and grow, b) people desire to build dynasties that extend their power and create a type of immortality, c) the use of rational and efficient methods are the best way to measure performance, d) capitalism and efficiency take precedence over human dignity (consequently, people lose sight of their morals), e) a matrix of organizations, interests, and resources is needed for growth, f) punishing people is good financial business and creates many jobs, and g) profiteers are not held accountable for their faulty products and their low quality services.

Social Constructionist Orientation

The social constructionist orientation is based upon interpretivism, which has both subjective and objective qualities (Kraska, 2004). On the one hand, interpretivism is subjective and claims that reality and meanings are shaped via individual experiences, which are unique to each individual. On the other hand, interpretivism is objective and claims that individuals constantly negotiate their perceptions with other people with whom they associate, reflecting an intersubjective reality (Weber, 2004). Indeed, there is no one single truth; reality for each person is constructed relative to personal experiences based upon language, symbols, and the interactions with other individuals (Kraska).

According to the social constructionist orientation, the purpose of the criminal justice system is socially constructed and depends on the political climate, social sentiment, cultural values, intellectual perspective, and interests of those in power (Kraska, 2004). Using the media to manage the appearance of the system's legitimacy, the public is continually bombarded with myths until the myths become accepted as facts. The criminal justice system can provide the public with select information, which creates the perception that the status quo must be maintained. Police can effectively create their own jobs by persuading the public to support their current efforts.

The assumptions of the social constructionist orientation are a) police use myths to develop problems that do not really exist, which divert public attention away from the real problems in society (e.g., unemployment and discrimination), and b) the interests of people in power must be protected (Kraska, 2004). Using descriptive statistics and the media, who need exciting crime stories to sell their product, the police can provide the information needed to create moral panic. For example, the police chief can increase the crime rate by ordering the officers to file multiple charges for each case report or the police chief can reduce the crime rate by ordering the officers to file a single charge for each case report. By appearing to effectively react to a problem, which never really existed, the police can gain the public's support.

Late Modernity Orientation

According to the late modernity orientation, the purpose of the criminal justice system is to promote safety and security by effectively identifying and managing classes of people who are assessed to be a threat (Kraska, 2004). The "goal is not to eliminate crime but to make it tolerable through systematic coordination" (Kraska, p. 305-307). Late modernity is not concerned with the underlying causes of crime; rather, it uses statistics to assess risk levels of particular classes of people and then tries to control populations that are identified as high risk. By incarcerating the high risk groups of people, significant aggregate effects in crime can be realized. In other words, crime can be reduced by rearranging the type of people who are still out in the general population (i.e., it reduces the percentage of high risk people who are roaming around in free society).

The main assumptions of the late modernity orientation are that the state cannot provide effective overall security, that private persons need to invest in their own situational crime prevention programs, and that people rationally choose to commit crime (Kraska, 2004). Because situational crime prevention programs require financial resources to implement, this excludes many of the poor people (who end up being labeled as outsiders). Late modernity orientation supporters claim that these misfortunate people are responsible for their own fates. By classifying these misfortunate individuals as outsiders, the dominant classes can effectively control them without the dominant classes giving up their own freedoms. Indeed, authorities can effectively control these misfortunate people because incarceration is easy to implement, it results in immediate consequence, it has few political opponents, it relies on the existing system of regulations, and it leaves the fundamental social and economic systems intact.

Oppression Orientation

Oppression orientation claims that the state protects the interests of the elite and powerful while oppressing the disadvantaged and less powerful (Kraska, 2004). In other words, the state uses the law as a tool for the political repression of those groups that threaten state power. There is a struggle for power and the groups that attain the most power are the ones who dictate the law. According to the oppression orientation, the purpose of the criminal justice system is to control people who threaten the status quo. Groups who are less powerful politically, which include minorities, women, and the poor, are used as scapegoats for America's problems. By using scapegoats, society is able to overlook the underlying factors that actually cause significant social harm (e.g., unemployment and poverty).

The assumption of oppression orientation is that the criminal justice system has built in bias against minorities, women, and the poor (Kraska, 2004). Indeed, because laws in the U.S. are based on men's perspective, the laws are inherently biased. In short, the criminal justice system abuses its power through the practice of institutional racism, sexism, and classism.

Police Department Orientations Conclusion

How a police department judges good behavior will impact the department's actions. If a police department fails to provide complete and truthful information and destroys evidence in order to win a case, the department is making a statement, which reflects upper management. Indeed, upper management controls police policy. In short, anti-social police behaviors will undermine public trust.

Police Department Orientations		
Crime Control The overall goal is to control crime by arresting as many people as possible, as fast as possible, using as few resources as possible. Mistakes are acceptable; police are trustworthy and they only arrest the guilty. 	**Police Department Orientations** • **Rational** • **Crime Control** • **Due Process** • **System** • **Politics and Criminal Justice** • **Growth Complex** • **Social Constructionist** • **Late Modernity** • **Oppression**	**Police Department Orientations** **What is good police officer behavior?** *Police managers have different ideas of right and wrong in which to judge good police officer behavior. Consequently, different police department orientations answer the question, "What is good police officer behavior?" in different manners.*
Due Process Personal freedom is more valuable than absolute security. People have a right to legal representation; police need to prove case in court. Mistakes by the police are unacceptable. 	**Rational** Law enforcement is a business. Everyone agrees to give up some freedom for peace and security. If the cost for crime is high enough, individuals will rationally choose to obey the law. 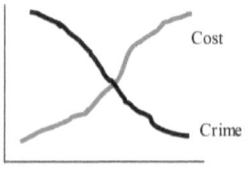	

Figure 2. Police Department Orientations.

Police Department Orientations		
System	**Growth Complex**	**Late Modernity**
Independent agencies work together to collect deviants, to transform them, and to return them to society. Public safety can be achieved through inter-agency cooperation and efficient operation of each agency.	Purpose of police is to build an ever growing bureaucracy. Police rules become the standard to measure performance (quotas). Police create problems to ensure jobs. Human dignity is unimportant; punishing individuals is profitable.	Purpose of police is to use statistics to assess risk levels and to promote safety by controlling the classes of people who have been identified as the problem. Individuals need to take responsibility to protect themselves.
		Crime Rate of Targeted Class
Politics	**Social Constructionist**	**Oppression**
Purpose of police depends on who has political power. Right wing: system is too lenient; left wing: system is too controlling.	Purpose of police is based on interpretivism. Good behavior is determined by culture, by social sentiment, and by people in power. Because there is no single truth, police use media to create myths.	Purpose of police is to protect the elite and powerful while controlling the disadvantaged and less powerful. The police should maintain the status quo by controlling minorities.
		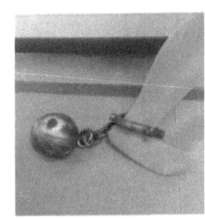

Figure 2 (continued). Police Department Orientations.

References

Brinkerhoff, J.R. (2009). *Domestic Operational Law: The Posse Comitatus Act and Homeland Security.* Retrieved from http:// usacac.army.mil/cac2/call/docs/10-16/ch_12.asp

Cain, W. (2003). Declaring independence. *Society, 41* (1).

Carter, D. (2002). *Issues in police-community relations: Taken from The Police and the community* (7th ed.). Boston, MA: Pearson Custom.

Dreisbach, C. (2008). *Ethics in criminal justice.* Boston, MA: McGraw-Hill Irwin.

Christian Police & Prison Association (n.d.). Retrieved from http:// cpa-usa.org/law-officers/canons-of-police-ethics/

Hames, J., and Ekern, Y. (2005). *Constitutional law: Principles and practice.* Clifton Park, NY: Thomson Delmar Learning.

Harberfeld, M.R. (2006). *Police leadership.* Upper Saddle River, NJ: Pearson Prentice.

Hess, K.M., & Bennett, W.W. (2007). *Management and supervision in law enforcement* (5th ed.). Belmont, CA: Wadsworth Thomson.

Kraska, P. (2004). *Theorizing criminal justice: Eight essential orientations.* Long Grove, IL: Waveland Press, Inc.

Perez, D.W., & Moore, J.A. (2002). *Police ethics: A matter of character.* Incline Village, NV: Copperhouse.

Pollock, J.M. (2004). *Ethics in crime and justice: Dilemmas & decisions.* Belmont, CA: Thomas-Wadsworth.

Reaves, B.A. (2007). Census of state and local law enforcement agencies, 2004. *Bureau of Justice Statistics Bulletin.* Retrieved from http://bjs.ojp.usdoj.gov/index.cfm?ty=dcdetail&iid=249

U.S. Department of Labor, Bureau of Labor Statistics (2009). *Occupational outlook handbook, 2010-11 edition.* Retrieved from http://www.bls.gov//oco/ocos/60.htm

Weber, R. (2004). The rhetoric of positivism versus interpretivism: A personal view. *MIS Quarterly 28*(1), iii-xii.

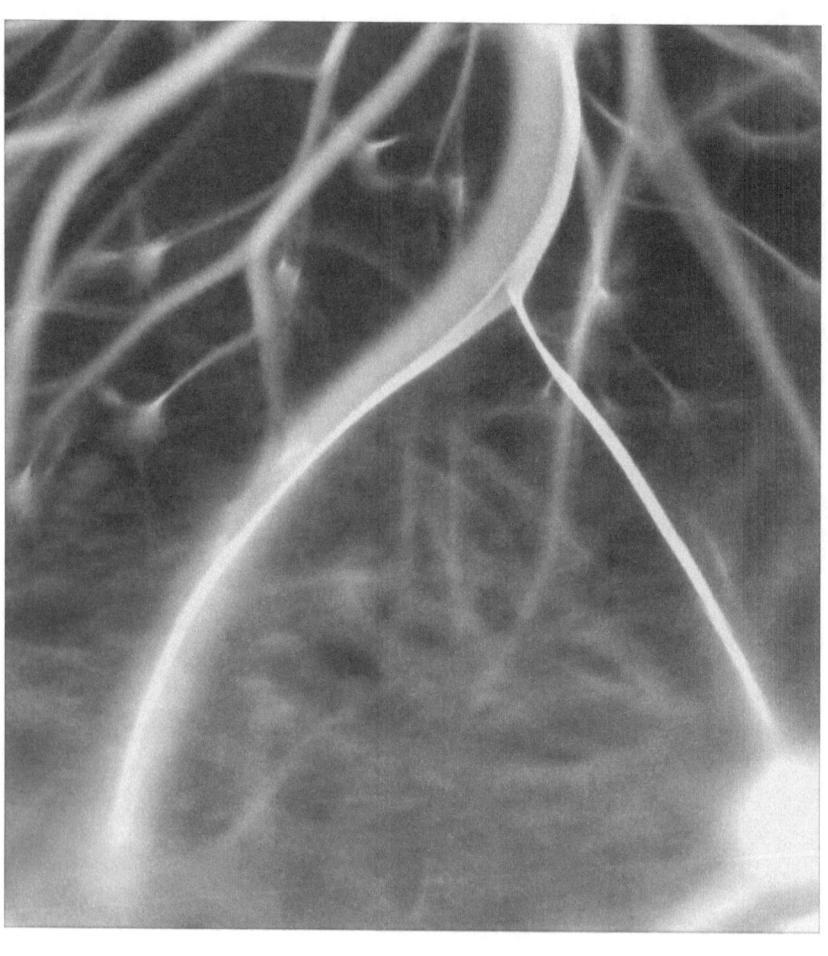

www.ingramcontent.com/pod-product-compliance
Lightning Source LLC
Chambersburg PA
CBHW030540290526
45786CB00004B/1795